Deadly SNAKES

Gareth Stevens
Publishing

Please visit our Web site www.garethstevens.com. For a free color catalog of all our high-quality books, call toll free 1-800-542-2595 or fax 1-877-542-2596.

Library of Congress Cataloging-in-Publication Data

Jackson, Tom, 1972-
  Deadly snakes / Tom Jackson.
     p. cm. — (Dangerous animals)
  Includes index.
  ISBN 978-1-4339-4041-5 (pbk.)
  ISBN 978-1-4339-4042-2 (6-pack)
  ISBN 978-1-4339-4040-8 (library binding)
  1. Snakes—Juvenile literature. I. Title.
  QL666.O6J258 2011
  597.96—dc22
                                    2010005858

Published in 2011 by
Gareth Stevens Publishing
111 East 14th Street, Suite 349
New York, NY 10003

© 2011 The Brown Reference Group Ltd.

For Gareth Stevens Publishing:
Art Direction: Haley Harasymiw
Editorial Direction: Kerri O'Donnell

For The Brown Reference Group Ltd:
Editorial Director: Lindsey Lowe
Managing Editor: Tim Harris
Editor: Tom Jackson
Children's Publisher: Anne O'Daly
Design Manager: David Poole
Designer: Aki Nakayama
Picture Manager: Sophie Mortimer
Production Director: Alastair Gourlay

Picture Credits:
Front Cover: Mary Evans Picture Library

Corbis: W. A. Raymondk: 17; istockphoto: 7b, 29bl; Henrick: 36; Hulton Archive; 8, 14; Timeflight: 35; Jupiter Images: Photos.com: 5, 9, 11b, 13, 15t, 16, 18, 19, 23b, 25, 26, 27i, 29t , 30-31, 31 b, 32, 33, 34b, 37, 38b, 39b, 40, 41, 43, 44, 45t; Stockxpert: 7t, 10, 11t, 15b, 21, 22, 34t, 42, 45b; Shutterstock: Concettina D' Agnese

All Artworks Brown Reference Group

Printed in the United States of America
1 2 3 4 5 6 7 8 9 12 11 10

CPSIA compliance information: Batch #CS10GS: For further information contact Gareth Stevens, New York, New York at 1-800-542-2595.

CONTENTS

Any words that appear in the text in **bold** are explained in the glossary.

WHAT IS A SNAKE?

Almost half of all **reptiles** are snakes. There are 3,000 different **species** that live all over the world—only Antarctica and a few islands are snake-free. All snakes are hunters and about a third of them kill with **venom**.

It might not look like it, but being snake-shaped is very useful. It lets the reptiles live and hunt in many different places. Tree snakes are usually long and thin so they can stretch across the gaps between branches. Burrowing snakes have smooth, rounded bodies for slithering through soil. Some snakes are brightly colored to stand out from the crowd, but most have blotches, bands, or stripes that break up their outline and give them extra **camouflage**.

This boa's scales have a dull pattern that helps keep the snake hidden from its victims.

Skinned Alive!

All snakes are covered in **scales**. Scales are tough plates that protect the body, but they cannot stretch much. A growing snake has to shed old skin when it gets too tight.

Although they do not have legs, snakes have no difficulty getting around. Most snakes move across the ground by wriggling their bodies from side to side in a series of S-shaped curves. They swim in the same way. A snake can even climb up a tree trunk. It first grips the tree with the front part of its body and hoists up the back half. Next, it grips with the back half while the front reaches forward.

Snakes have poor eyesight and hearing but an excellent sense of smell. They do most of their smelling with their tongues! As it flicks, the tongue senses chemicals. This information is then passed to the snake's brain.

UP CLOSE

Some snakes have organs called pits on their faces. The pits pick up heat from warm-blooded animals, such as rats. The snake can use this heat signal to find prey even in total darkness.

ANACONDA

The green anaconda is the world's mightiest snake. The females grow very large, big enough to kill a deer or even a fully grown caiman. They have few enemies.

Large adult anacondas are too heavy to slither far on land. They spend most of the time in swamps and rivers, where the water supports their bodies. They lie in wait for prey, ready to explode into action should an animal stray within range. Once it has captured an animal, the anaconda wraps it in several coils of its muscular body—and squeezes tight.

An anaconda has a narrow head with both its eyes and its **nostrils** near the top. A bold black line runs diagonally backward from each of the anaconda's eyes to its jaw.

Head

Tail

Scales

Mating Snakes

Anacondas usually mate in shallow water. A "ball" of a dozen males crawl over one female, trying to mate with her. The little male snakes need to be careful. Their mate might try to eat them!

Common name:
anaconda
Scientific name:
Eunectes murinus
Length: Up to 33 ft (10 m)
Key features: massive, greenish body with dark oval spots; thick neck; females more than twice as long as males
Diet: **mammals** (including deer, chickens, and dogs), birds, other reptiles; young anacondas eat fish and frogs

CHILDREN'S

You might think that with a name like this, a Children's python would make a good pet. But watch out! This snake is not very cuddly. It is actually named for a zookeeper who lived in the 1800s.

Children's pythons are often seen hanging around near the mouths of caves. They are waiting for bats to come out in the evening. As the crowd of bats streams out, the snakes lunge forward with their mouths open to snatch one from midair. As soon as it catches a bat, a snake crushes it with its coils and swallows it while still hanging upside down!

Tail

Scales

Eye

Many Homes

Children's pythons live in the far north of Australia. They live in many different areas, including rain forests, dry woodlands, and desert cliffs.

PYTHON

Common name: Children's python
Scientific name: Antaresia childreni
Length: can grow up to 3.3 ft (1 m) long
Key features: small and slender with large yellow eyes; light brown body with lots of darker brown blotches on the back and sides
Diet: small mammals and birds; other reptiles

UP CLOSE

A female Children's python lays a group, or clutch, of about nine eggs. She coils her body around them and stays with her eggs until the babies hatch.

RAINBOW

The rainbow boa of Central and South America is a secretive creature! It stays hidden away in the rain forest all day, but comes out to hunt in the branches as night falls.

The rainbow boa's head is narrow, and there are nearly always five dark lines running from the snout and down the head. The markings on the snake's back are black or dark brown oval rings. Normally the centers of the ovals are lighter than the rest of the scales, and some snakes have eye-shaped spots on their sides.

Night Attack!

A rainbow boa hunts in the dark. On its snout are organs called heat pits. These can detect the heat given off by animals. The heat sensors can even find victims hiding among leaves.

Scales

Tail

Mouth

Head

BOA

Common name:
rainbow boa
Scientific name:
Epicrates cenchria
Length: from 5 ft
(1.5 m) to 6.5 ft (2 m)
Key features:
powerful body with glossy
scales
Diet: mostly mammals

UP CLOSE

When a rainbow boa comes
out into the sunlight, its
beautiful scales shimmer
with every color of the
rainbow. This is how
the snake gets
its name.

11

KING
COBRA

The king cobra is the longest poisonous snake in the world—and one of the deadliest. Its venom can kill a person, but cobras prefer to eat other snakes.

King cobras live in southern Asia, and they often turn up close to towns and villages. They may be deadly, but they are also shy snakes and normally slip away quietly rather than attack. That's just as well, because a bite from a cobra could kill you in half an hour. Hospital treatment can save your life, but thousands of people die from cobra bites each year before they can reach help.

Common name: king cobra
Scientific name: Ophiophagus hannah
Length: usually grows from 10 ft (3 m) to 16.5 ft (5 m), but can reach 18 ft (5.5 m)
Key features: yellow or green body with smooth scales; spreads its long, narrow hood when it is threatened
Diet: other snakes, sometimes lizards

UP CLOSE

When a king cobra is alarmed, it rears up into the air. At the same time, it spreads flaps of skin at its neck to form a scary "hood."

Hood

Tongue

In The Nest

King cobras are the only snakes that build a nest. The female pulls together a pile of dead leaves with her coils. Then she lays 20 to 40 eggs. She guards the eggs from **predators**.

Tail

Scales

SEA KRAIT

The sea krait cruises the shallow coral seas of Southeast Asia and Australia. This snake's venom is so powerful that it kills its victims in less than a minute!

Sea kraits spend most of their time in the water, but they have to come to the surface to breathe every few minutes. They cruise slowly over **coral reefs**, poking their heads into holes as they search for their favorite prey—eels. Sea kraits may drag their prey onto land to eat it, and they also need to slither out of the sea to find freshwater to drink.

Safe In A Cave

A female sea krait lays about 12 eggs at a time.
She chooses a cave that is above the high-tide
level so the eggs don't get washed away.
The young sea kraits hatch after
about four or five months.

Tail

Head

Scales

Eel

Common name: sea krait
Scientific name: Laticauda
Length: from 3 ft (91 cm)
to 6.5 ft (2 m)
Key features:
cylinder-shaped body except for
the tail, which is flattened; black
and white in color, with rings
around body and tail
Diet: mostly eels

UP CLOSE

The bold black-and-white
bands on a sea krait's body
warn predators that
the snake has a dangerous
bite. Even a shark won't
dare to attack a sea krait.

RUSSELL'S

Russell's vipers may look beautiful, but they are not nice! In Asia, they bite more people than any other snake. The bites hurt badly.

Strike out

Russell's vipers do not have heat pits, but there are heat-sensitive nerves on their faces. These can detect warm-blooded prey, such as rats, mice, and birds. Russell's vipers move slowly as they look for prey, but once in position they launch an attack in the blink of an eye.

Russell's vipers live in southern Asia. They like to take it easy, and lie coiled up in a sunny spot among the grass. They have good camouflage and lie ready and waiting to **ambush** any passing prey. At night they go out looking for food and often stray into villages. If the snakes are spooked, they hiss through their large nostrils and will bite if cornered.

Scales

Nostril

Head

Tail

VIPER

UP CLOSE

The viper's **fangs** are about 0.5 inch (1.3 cm) long and can inject venom deep into a victim. But snakes do not waste venom, and most bites contain only small amounts of poison.

Common name: Russell's viper

Scientific name: Daboia russelii

Length: from 36 in (90 cm) to 5 ft (1.5 m) long

Key features: round, brown spots edged in black on body; dark stripe runs from eye to corner of jaw

Diet: mammals, such as rats, mice, and squirrels; birds, such as sparrows; lizards and frogs

WESTERN DIAMO RATTLESNA

The western diamondback rattlesnake is the deadliest snake in North America. Its bite can kill, so listen out for its warning r-r-rattle!

Rattlesnakes don't use their rattles to confuse their prey, or to attract other rattlesnakes! In fact, the rattle is like a warning alarm to let other animals know a grumpy rattlesnake is close by. Huge herds of bison once roamed the plains of North America. Rattlesnakes shook their rattles to drive the bison away. The scary sound stopped the animals from trampling on the snakes!

Rattle

Scales

Head

UP CLOSE

A rattlesnake's rattle is made of keratin, a hard substance that also forms horns, nails, claws, and hair. The pieces of the rattle fit neatly together, one inside the other.

BACK

Common name: western diamondback
Scientific name: *Crotalus atrox*
Length: From 2.5 ft (76 cm) to 7 ft (2.1 m)
Key features: diamond-shaped markings along back of body; tail banded in black, ending in the rattle
Diet: rats and small mammals up to the size of young prairie dogs and rabbits

Snake Snack!

The western diamondback rattlesnake lives in deserts, on rocky hillsides, and in other dry places where there are plenty of small **rodents** to eat!

SIDEWIND

The sidewinder is a rattlesnake that gets its name from the way it slithers. It lives in deserts and has to throw its body sideways to move over the loose sand!

Sidewinders don't have a home. They are always on the move, heading out across the desert each night, looking for lizards asleep in their burrows. At dawn, the snakes shuffle down into the sand to escape the heat. They hide under a thin layer of sand so that they can surprise any prey, such as lizards or jumping rats, that pass by.

Tricky Tails

Baby sidewinders use their tail to attract lizards. The babies move their tail slowly across the sand so the segments look like a crawling insect. As a lizard comes close, the snake strikes.

Horn

Tail

Scales

Common name: sidewinder
Scientific name: Crotalus cerastes
Length: from 1.5 ft (46 cm) to 2.5 ft (76 cm)
Key features: scales above eyes look like horns;
body is smaller and slimmer than other rattlesnakes
Diet: mainly lizards and small desert
rodents, such as rats and mice, and
occasionally birds

UP CLOSE

The sidewinder has
scales that bulge out above
its eyes like a pair
of horns. This is why some
people call sidewinders
"horned rattlesnakes."

PUFF ADD

The puff adder is a huge, scary snake from Africa. It looks even larger when it is angry—it puffs itself up like a balloon by sucking in air. The snake then slowly lets the air out to make a spine-chilling hiss.

An adult puff adder is so bulky that it cannot move from side to side like other snakes. Instead, it travels slowly in a straight line, a bit like a caterpillar. This snake hunts at dusk when it is harder for other animals to see it move. Puff adders often leap into the air as they strike a victim, and may even topple over backward. The wide head contains big tanks, or glands, of venom under the eyes.

Tricky Tales

Puff adders eat rats, birds, toads, and other snakes. They will even eat African hedgehogs and tortoises—which they swallow whole! The snake only injects venom into large prey.

Scales

Head

Mouth

22

UP CLOSE

A puff adder's scales are rough, with a raised ridge running along the middle. The ridges work like the tread on tires and help the snake grip the ground.

Common name: puff adder

Scientific name: *Bitis arietans*

Length: from 3 ft (90 cm) to 6 ft (1.8 m)

Key features: plump body; raised ridge on each scale; large, dark gray v-shaped marks along the back

Diet: birds, toads, lizards, and mammals, including small antelopes and tortoises

TAIPAN

Most taipans live near the coasts of Australia, but the ones inland are the most dangerous. A bite from a taipan contains more than enough venom to kill several humans in minutes!

Taipans have very long fangs. They use them to bite their prey. Poisonous venom is squirted through the fangs and into their victim. Despite this, taipans are shy and rarely bite people.

Head

Tail

Mouth

Common name: taipan
Scientific name: Oxyuranus
Length: 6.5 ft (2 m) to 12 ft (3.6 m)
Key features: large, tube-shaped body; narrow head; usually some shade of brown in color
Diet: mammals, mostly rats, one of the few rodents in the dry Australian desert

Poison Power

Inland taipans are known as fierce snakes. They are the most **venomous** snakes of all. A single bite injects enough poison to kill 200,000 mice!

UP CLOSE

All taipans have a very fast and accurate bite. This means that a taipan can quickly inject its deadly venom into its victim and kill it.

AUSTRALIAN TIGER SNAKE

The tiger snake is one of the world's most venomous snakes. But if you are unlucky enough to be bitten by one, modern medicines will save your life if you get to the hospital quickly!

When a tiger snake is annoyed, it flattens its neck and raises its head off the ground like a cobra. And it will bite you if it gets the chance—often on the legs. However, a tiger snake's bite is unlikely to kill you. Its poison can be treated with **antivenin** (also called antivenom). Most people don't take any chances, though: they wear clothes that cover their legs.

Tail

Head

Scales

Common name: Australian tiger snake
Scientific name: Notechis scutatus
Length: from 4 ft (1.2 m) to 7 ft (2.1 m)
Key features: plump body with large scales; large head with a blunt nose and small eyes
Diet: mostly frogs; also lizards, birds, and small mammals, such as rats

Snake Sizes

A tiger snake's size depends on the size of its food! Large ones eat big seabirds and rats. Medium-sized snakes eat smaller birds and mice. The smallest tiger snakes eat little lizards.

UP CLOSE

Tiger snakes swallow frogs whole, without waiting for their venom to work. However, a tiger snake will release larger prey (such as a rat) after biting it. The snake will then follow the dying animal and eat it later.

MAMBA

Mambas are dangerous snakes that attack without warning. The largest type, the black mamba, is also the fastest snake in the world. It can slither faster than a man can run!

All mambas live in Africa. Most are green and stay hidden in tall trees. The black mamba lives on grassy plains. Mamba venom is very powerful. Luckily, the snakes prefer to hide rather than attack people.

Snake Fight!

Male black mambas often wrestle each other as they compete for mates. Each snake lifts up to half of its body off the ground. He wraps it around his opponent and tries to push him over.

Tree

Tail

Head

Common name: mamba
Scientific name: Dendroaspis
Length: from 5 ft (1.5 m) to 14 ft (4.3 m)
Key features: long, slim body with smooth scales; can be green, gray, or brown; never black except inside mouth
Diet: rodents, bats, and baby birds

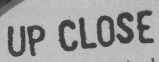

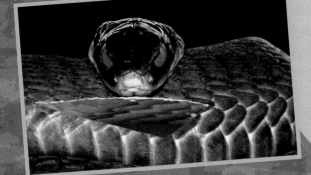

UP CLOSE

A black mamba's dark coloring helps it to stay hidden in rocks and hollow tree trunks. It also takes in heat from the sun better than pale skin, so the snake warms up quickly.

GLOSSARY

ambush To attack suddenly from a hidden place.

antivenin A substance made from snake venom that is used to treat snakebites.

caiman A kind of crocodile that lives in the tropical parts of the Americas. Caimans are closely related to alligators.

camouflage A coloring or body shape that helps an animal to blend with and hide in its surroundings.

coral reef A line of coral that lies below the water in warm, shallow seas. Coral is made up of tiny animals.

fang A long, pointed tooth. Some snakes use their fangs to inject venom.

mammal An animal that is warm-blooded and feeds its young with its own milk. Most mammals also have hair or fur.

nostril An opening in the nose through which an animal or person breathes.

predator An animal that hunts other animals for food.

prey An animal that is hunted by another animal.

reptile An animal with scaly skin. A reptile is cold-blooded, which means that its temperature varies with its surroundings.

rodent A small mammal, such as a rat or mouse, with large teeth.

scales Tough, waterproof coverings that grow out of a snake's skin. The scales protect the snake's body while letting it stretch and bend.

snout An animal's nose and jaws.

species A group of animals that sha features. Members of the same spec can mate and produce young togeth

venom A poisonous liquid that som snakes produce. They inject the pois into their victims by biting with the fangs.

venomous Capable of producing venom.

warm-blooded An animal that car keep its body at about the same temperature all the time. People, r and birds are all warm-blooded.

FURTHER RESOURCES

Books about snakes

Allman, Toney. *Vipers.* Farmington Hills, MI: KidHaven Press, 2005.

Bredeson, Carmen. *Boa Constrictors Up Close.* Berkeley Heights, NJ: Enslow Publishers, Inc., 2006.

Gray, Maurice. *Constrictors.* Farmington Hills, MI: KidHaven Press, 2005.

Hansen, Paul. *When Snakes Attack!* Berkeley Heights, NJ: Enslow Publishers, Inc., 2006.

White, Nancy. *King Cobras: The Biggest Venomous Snakes of All!* New York: Bearport Publishing Company, Inc., 2009.

Useful Web sites

American International Rattlesnake Museum
http://www.rattlesnakes.com/core.html

Animal Planet: Snake Facts and Pictures
http://animal.discovery.com/reptiles/snake

Snake Facts
http://www.kidzone.ws/lw/snakes/facts.htm

What's That Snake?
http://www.oplin.org/snake/